naked

sarah ciminillo

For Bianka
Happy Birthday! ♡

Love,
Sarah Ciminillo

sarah ciminillo

each one of these poems
had a purpose in my growth -
they were for me
and now they are for you

i see you growing
i see you trying
keep going
keep showing your emotions
and vulnerability
they are a part of you
and it's so
beautiful

naked

a special thanks
to my
flynn rider -
thank you
for believing
in me and
my dream

sarah ciminillo

contents

the heartbreaks
battling anxiety
self-love and healing
falling in love
quarantine journals

naked

the heartbreaks

sarah ciminillo

maybe since
the only example
of being in love
i've seen
is through movies
and books
then maybe
i'm not to blame
for expecting
a happy ending

- *divorced parents*

naked

a vicious cycle -

we normalize the disappearance of a parent
but sing about the heartbreak of a lover
and wonder why
we feel so alone

sarah ciminillo

i often forget about my father's ex wife
my memory of her is
fast
hard
gone
irrelevant
like the time she punched me
when i was twelve years old

i think about it
and i can't remember if it hurt
i remember her hand coming towards me
but that's it

i also remember
my father telling me
not to tell
anyone

somehow i understood
i understood because of her mental illness
and i still understand

and maybe that's why i don't remember the pain
and why i don't really care

naked

<u>life of an empath</u>

i'm an anchor
to everyone's boat load
of emotions
taking their sadness
their heaviness
down with me
nobody asked me to be
their anchor
but nonetheless
i'm in the sand
with grains of guilt
surrounding me

i am breaking my own heart

sarah ciminillo

i miss the days when i was a little girl
and i would wake with a natural hope
a genuine excitement about what the day will
bring me
i would get up
put a t-shirt and overalls on
run outside barefoot
slipping and gripping the mildew morning grass
all the way down to the dock
as the sun warmed up the earth
and my soul

naked

everyone talks about
a broken heart
because of a past lover
but no one talks about
a broken heart
because of a parent

and those of you
who know the feeling
know that it's more than
just a broken heart

it's a bruise that doesn't heal
it's an empty seat
it's catastrophe
it's half the holidays
it's a third of me
it's modern society

sarah ciminillo

<u>alternate rapunzel</u>

let's talk about it
the things that make you, *you*
i'll go first

locked away in a tower of traumas
there is a story
about a princess who was controlled
through her hair
yes, you read that correctly
her hair
she was never allowed to have long hair
strict orders from the king
she cried and wished
and imagined what it felt like to
have hair that touched her back
but she never got the chance
until the king moved away for good

so when people ask why i don't cut my hair
there's more to it than
i just like it long

naked

i ate a fried pickle
and it reminded me of one of my father's ex
girlfriends
she was chinese
and barely knew english
i taught her how to say lilypad
she used to cook with whatever we had in the
fridge

one night after fishing on our lake
we retired back to the house with a catfish
she cooked that catfish with

- garlic
- tofu
- pickles

it was actually delicious
those warm pickles with fresh catfish

and i'll never forget how i heard my father
screaming at her in the basement
similar to the way he screamed at me
i felt bad for her
how i watched him break her phone into two
pieces

how one morning all of her things

sarah ciminillo

and all of her

    were gone

naked

i'm afraid to see you
because i'm afraid i'll see my past self too
the one that was susceptible to fear
and never saw things clear;
feelings that you caused
and never said sorry for
feelings you don't know about
because you sought the door

i'm afraid to see you
because i think you'll be the same -
seeing life as one big game

sarah ciminillo

you don't get to see
the post-apocalyptic version of me
not after the chaos you created

scraped up from the ashes
i became something
that i am proud of
something that you cannot break

what's that saying?
you break it, you buy it
you broke our relationship
which bought you
your reality

my absence

naked

like the lake after a storm
everything is fine now
smooth - you can tell that something happened
but there's things about it now
that are even more beautiful
than before
seashells and lilypads washed up
on shore

- *the aftermath*

sarah ciminillo

the *quiet girl* had more things to worry about

my father's car would pull in
and i prepared myself
for a lot of yelling
his heated words burned his own hands
in a custody battle
and spread like wildfire
destroying any chance of opportunity
leaving wounds that i, *a child*,
was supposed to *fix*
many tears
and endless amounts of guilt
oh, the hopeless
meaningless
guilt
forced upon my little human self
i didn't know better
just that i wanted my parents to be happy
so that i could be

- *why i dreaded leaving school yet didn't belong*

naked

<u>lost hopes</u>

i haven't seen
a future with you
in quite some time
just ask my dreams

they haven't seen you either

sarah ciminillo

not one word
was said
between us
but i thought
a thousand

who knew that
walking past
one person
would make me feel
like i have open
wounds on a
salty sidewalk
and leave my personality
feeling cold

who knew that
i could still
envision her
belongings on
my side of the room
and left over red hairs
on my blue pillow

who knew
that cheating
opens a part
of you that you

naked

tried so hard
to move on from

who knew you
could dislike
a name

sarah ciminillo

"i like your wings"
he said

as his actions
washed them
off

naked

i'm uncomfortable
but if i leave
i will be
uncomfortable

- *break-ups aren't meant to be a breeze*

sarah ciminillo

you say the cards
are in my hands
but i'm still learning
how to play
i've never been good at games
or trusting
what people say

- *don't tell me; show me*

naked

but
i cannot tell someone
how to love me
just like i cannot tell them
what a poem means to them

i have to wait for love to align
that part in the poem to rhyme

sarah ciminillo

we mustn't act upon
what isn't said
those are obstacles
that only exist in our head

act upon
what is
and what a person does
it's okay to be sad
about what once was

- *wishing he'd say what i want to hear*

naked

missing you
feels like
a personal hell
i have fallen
under your spell

- *there's no breaking it; just the breaking of me*

sarah ciminillo

the best decisions
are never
the easiest
but easy is
what we want
so we settle

- *comfortable*

naked

<u>manipulation hooks</u>

the hardest part
about letting you go
is knowing that you need
someone like me
in your life
someone who loves you
regardless of your
negligent words
and habits
someone who knows that
you're more than what
your flaws portray
someone who has seen you naked
with your clothes on
someone like me
who knows that you
flourish in soft
and selfless love
and that is why i am sad
you demolished
your shot at everything
you needed

sarah ciminillo

i would
have
loved you
forever
and here
i am
still loving
you

naked

<u>a mirage</u>

loving you
made my soul hot
like the desert
and was as
breathtaking as
a mirage

but that's all
it was;
a mirage
and when i
came out of it
i realized that
somewhere along
the scenic route
i stepped into
quicksand

baby, you were
the quicksand
but i couldn't take
my eyes off
the mirage
so there i was -
mesmerized
thirsty

sarah ciminillo

distracted

and sinking

naked

we hurt each other
in ways that was
the opposite of love
and sometimes i wonder
if we're to blame
or if it was the time fillers

the drinking
the phones
the parties

and if they didn't exist
that maybe we would
still be together

and then i realized
that i'm still making excuses for you
that i'm using those fillers to cover up the deep
cuts
when i need to let them breathe and heal
let them be what they are

- *acceptance*

i'm sorry
that i'm not who you thought
i was
or who you wanted me to be
that i said things
that aren't true at this point in time anymore
i meant them
the past version of me meant them

and if feelings
are like seasons
then i did fall
but i was shedding pieces of myself
growing colder
my environment was changing
but i was not

and i'm sorry
that i was unable
to flourish in your element

naked

i think missing you
is a bad thing
i think that i shouldn't by now
that i shouldn't feel anything
at all
but i do
i miss you

i should stop torturing myself
with the idea that it's bad
and start freeing myself
with the idea that it's true

i miss you

it doesn't have to mean more
or less
i need to stop telling myself that i'm a mess

sarah ciminillo

cut ties with the person
who only texts you
when they're drunk

you're worth more
than a lousy bar tab
that they racked up
just to acquire the thought
of talking to you

naked

you've been with people
who made your body feel like
a conquest
a map to treasure
but *their* treasure
and didn't share any of it with you
only their glory did they share
and then they left you

just hold on sweet thing
the right person will see you as treasure
and then map out the rest of their life with you

sarah ciminillo

my coffee doesn't wake me up like it used to
those feel good songs only sound like a series of words
nothing is pleasing my soul -
that stubborn taurus bull

and i'm looking the other way when i see my sad reflection
denying it's presence

the sun doesn't feel as good
those yellows and blues
remind me of the lack of *hellos* from you

i'm trying to rationalize
and think objectively
but the fact is
i miss you madly

i didn't know your lips and everything they do held this magic
i feel like i'm living through sleeping beauty's tragic
asleep through my days
until i see your face

i feel empty
with a gut wrenching anger

naked

you were never mine but i was yours
and now i feel your love in my pores
but to say that wouldn't be totally true
we were each other's
sharing
loving
and just being

meeting you
led to something
neither of us had
foreseen
and now
everything i do

i
feel
you

sarah ciminillo

my heart is struggling
and maybe that's because
it's pulling the weight
of other people's feelings
with only a few
delicate strings

naked

<u>cut your losses</u>

it's never been easy cutting my hair
i'm afraid i won't like it
that the hair stylist will mess up
that i'll miss my long hair

and a lot of times i'm like this with my relationships
when i really just need to chop off the dead ends
it's not helping me grow
it's just making it harder to brush through and maintain

getting little trims feels better
and those dead ends never miss me

sarah ciminillo

we live in a world
where our feelings
are only communicated
through fingers and screens
yet we're not supposed to wonder
what it all means
we just keep up a facade
and hope that it's not
a waste of time
once it's social media official
only then can i call you mine

naked

when you seek something out, it never ends up being what you need, and later you'll find out that it wasn't what you truly wanted either. it was the idea that you wanted, and you thought you saw what you needed in it too. and that's okay, but that's where we mess up; we expected so much out of something that just wasn't meant to be. developing expectations that were never possible to be reached in the first place.

sarah ciminillo

<u>robots</u>

to be totally honest
i have no clue how to
hook up with someone
and have it be just that

we're using each other's
bodies and time
but what about our minds?
the very thing that drives it all
don't you wonder about things?

when you kiss my body
do you ever think about
what i did that day?
when you run your fingers
through my hair
do you picture the way
the sun hits it?
or how about when i tell
you something that made
me laugh
do you notice the way
my eyes smile too?

do people care like i do?

naked

<u>one hit wonders</u>

how ironic is it
that most of our muses
never even began
to amuse us -
but amused the tools
in which we use to create
something they will never appreciate

sarah ciminillo

a beautiful rose
her color pleasing to the eye
picked then left to die

naked

<u>a pit of poetry</u>

thank you to my muses
for the excuses
but also the desire
because i threw it all
into a fire
and made a pit of poetry
sometimes it burns
but nonetheless

it keeps me warm

sarah ciminillo

<u>happy hour</u>

i want to be more
than a drunk kiss
more than a check
on a list
i want to be
the time
on your wrist

naked

i think people are afraid
to admit that they are better
with someone
they want to feel capable
like they can take on this world alone

but this world is scary
and i'll be the first to admit
that i do
need someone

sarah ciminillo

a book on a shelf
wanting hands around herself
offering her mind

- *rarely is it enough*

naked

you said you would've
done anything for me -
"given me every penny"

and that's how i knew we were different
because you cared about the penny
and i cared about the luck
of finding it

dead rose

it is demeaning
whenever someone says
"you can do better anyways"

they don't know
the joy
the passion
the friendship
you gave me

- *tell me, what's better than that?*

naked

our hearts are kind of unfair
they keep us alive
but they surely beat for another
pumping both sadness
and passion
through our bodies
holding us hostage to
what was
and what isn't

sarah ciminillo

we've turned into my
seashell collection
something i keep tucked away
but something i'll always see
as a treasure
something that i'm happy i once found

naked

battling anxiety

dating with anxiety

i'm sorry
for looking away so quickly
and asking you to repeat
what you just said
i've just been anxious
since the moment i left my bed
i promise that i'm interested
and that i care
don't pay attention
to how many times i touch my hair

i'm trying to escape
the prison inside my head
my hands are freezing - am i dead?
my symptoms are overwhelming
and i'm running out
of things to do
i want to tell you
if only you knew

i want to cut the night short
because i'm afraid
afraid of my body
and what would happen if i stayed
the tingling numbness sets in
and i know the attack is almost done

naked

and then i'm just proud
that for once i didn't run

alone but not

there's something
under my bed
it's not a monster
but rather
insecurities
that do seem
monstrous
and sometimes
they come out
from under my bed
when they know
that i'm alone
and feeling
vulnerable

naked

anxiety is
your body forcing you
to walk to the edge
and then not jumping

straining your muscles
stealing your breath
you're the walking dead

you don't know where
you're going
your focus is on
the symptoms you're showing

and then you slowly back up
and start to remember
your name
and you can't help
but feel a little insane

sarah ciminillo

<u>society is stealing my sleep</u>

what's wrong with me?
i ask myself
as i rub my tired, puffy eyes
a long night of my body
rejecting sleep
because of the rejection
it receives

naked

<u>museum of bad habits</u>

our bodies are works of art
yet we treat them like
they're not one of a kind

sarah ciminillo

my body is lying to me
it's acting like i just went for a run
even though i've been in bed for two hours
my hands are tingling
as if they think they have super powers
but they don't

they have no power at all
just a pen
and some paper

naked

so go to that pity party
but remember that you have to drive yourself
home later

sarah ciminillo

someone asks me
"what's your story?"

i look down at my hands and feet
thinking about what they've conquered and
seen
i wonder, what do they mean?
and how far back are they talking?
i feel hot flashes in my face and chest
memories that manifest
an accelerated heartbeat
i didn't just grow up in one spot
i don't just have one story - not one straight line

finally i look up at this person i hardly know
and all i can manage is a feeling of

i don't really know

a generation of misfits

we feel lost
perhaps it has to do with our dependence
on being heard and seen by others
because if we are not, then what will we do?
who will cheer us on?
we've convinced ourselves that we can't possibly
do that alone
we worry about how many people like our
company
we try to move on, when we actually don't
we say we need a drink and then feel ourselves
sink back into what is comfortable
we wake up and check on what others are doing
we watch people's stories
and compare their days with ours
we don't feel like we do enough
and when we do, we make sure everyone knows
about it
because we care more about what people think
than actually living
we preach about self-care and mental health
but stare at a phone screen for most of our day
blocking our path right in front of us
stealing our sight of what we want for our
futures

sarah ciminillo

we're imprisoned by shackles made of phone chargers
we can't figure out our dreams because we have yet to wake up
we're so afraid to make a decision that we wait for the cold world decide for us
and wonder why we remain so unsatisfied

yet we ask -
why do we feel so lost?

naked

<u>car therapy</u>

i don't know why i'm crying
maybe because all michigan has done is rained
maybe because my umbrella of safety has a hole
or two in it
maybe it's that last drink i had
maybe i'm just having a moment
or maybe being human means crying alone in
the car sometimes

sarah ciminillo

let go. let go of that image of yourself in your head that isn't true; or contributing to your life right now. you're not late, you're not early. you are exactly where you're supposed to be. every decision that you have made, has led you to this very moment - and it is up to you if you like it or not. if you don't like it, it was still your destiny and you didn't do one thing wrong. you have the power to make your life exactly what you want it to be. everyone has a passion inside of them, and each one of them can be ignited. forget the idea of how things are "supposed" to be. maybe at one point things were supposed to be different and you feel underachieved because you didn't reach that plan. it happens; in fact, plans rarely work out exactly how we envision them in our minds, and that's okay. give yourself a break, because if you worked hard and gave it your all, then you did not fail. don't keep painting on the same piece of paper, when at this point you're putting way too much paint on it and it's a soggy mess. get a new piece of paper, and start a new project.

naked

anxiety is
pacing and standing near the door
when someone says they're almost there
anxiety is
the instant regret
when you commit to future plans
anxiety is
that pounding heartbeat
when someone calls you
how should i sound when i answer?
i hate the way i say *"hello"* so i don't, i say
"yellow"
anxiety is
the prickly spritz of fear
when someone says my name
anxiety is
when i'm in a large crowd
and i'm too aware of how i'm sitting, what i'm
doing with my hands
thinking that everyone is watching and judging
me
anxiety is
a bitch with nothing better to do

sarah ciminillo

<u>my poor wet pillow</u>

i hate feeling
sorry for myself
because i then
have to convince
myself that
it's going
to be okay

naked

i'm driving
my body's service engine light comes on
and it looks a lot like a breaking car

shaking
leaking water
the air doesn't work
it takes you longer to get to where you need to
go

i don't know how to fix it
and i guess i didn't have to because then there
was a hand
gently holding my cold, sweaty hand as if it
didn't feel like a dead fish
and suddenly i was out of the tunnel
i could breathe

where did i just go?

sarah ciminillo

she tries to be
black and white
but her tears
produce
a grey runoff

- *some things aren't that simple*

naked

you can really mess yourself up
when you try too hard to keep a smile on your face
you start to accept the evil in your life
you make excuses for it
you justify it
until it becomes a norm
you think that you can be strong enough to go against - and you are
but going against a river eventually tires out your legs

and then you start to believe that this is what life is now

it's not

let the river take you
let the water run down your face
let it rush you over the edge

let nature give you your new beginning
that you deserve

sarah ciminillo

the stages of anxiety

1. *popcorn brain* - this is when my thoughts are jumbled and i'm thinking of many things at once

2. *one-track mind* - this is when the "doomsday" cloud mellows out my popcorn brain with fears that i know are irrational

3. *pounding heart and sweaty hands* - this doesn't always occur together but for me, sometimes it does

4. *heavy, airless chest* - this is the worst part for me, because i then get too much in my head with the obvious fact that i can't breathe. i start to self-diagnose

5. *hot body* - i typically feel it in my face

6. *stiff, numb hands* - this part is slow going and it feels like my hands are shutting down. the first time this happened to me, i thought i was having a stroke and begged my sister to take me to the

hospital

7. *uncontrolled crying* - this is the last step, and thus, a love/hate relationship with me because i know that the attack is over

sarah ciminillo

<u>the remedies</u>

1. *something cold to drink* - try to avoid anything with caffeine; it will accelerate your heart rate and make you freak out even more

2. *an open space* - typically going outside is my go-to

3. *walking* - if i'm at stage four in my anxiety, usually walking outside is the only thing that will help me at that point. shifting your focus to exercising and the beauty of nature is a great way to distract your mind from spiraling

4. *spilling your thoughts to someone or something* - if my sister isn't around to let me talk her ear off, that's when i turn to my journal. once the thoughts are out, i can start to see what's bothering me and then decide for myself if it's worth the panic, and work on seeking solutions

5. *stretching* - this is a new technique i started trying out once i got to stage four in my anxiety. stretching out my

arms and opening my torso helped me
overcome the feeling of being unable to
breathe

6. *doing an activity, such as cleaning* - i had
   popcorn brain one day and couldn't
   organize my emotions, so i started to
   organize my bathroom and it distracted
   me. once i was finished, i felt better. i
   felt like i physically worked out my
   distress by cleaning a mess

what doesn't help

1. *when someone is having an attack*, it is not the time to ask them *why* they're having one. do you ask someone why they're having a heart attack? probably not. try to avoid people who have the tendency of doing that when you feel an attack coming on

2. *empty stomach* - most of my attacks tend to come on when i haven't eaten, and/or drank water. make sure you have a healthy body, so that you can have a healthy mind too

3. *sometimes, alcohol* - this one is tricky. on one hand, alcohol is a good way for me to calm down in social gatherings and dates. however, the hangover is what induces my attacks. it's definitely a double-edged sword

4. *an uncomfortable environment* - if i'm experiencing anxiety in an environment that i don't want to be in - such as an awkward family event, social gathering, a meeting, or small area - it doesn't help.

naked

if my body can't freely move, it intensifies the attack. the car is usually the worst place for me, because it's crowded and the air doesn't seem like it's circulating. so if i'm experiencing anxiety, i make sure to prepare myself before getting in the car with some cold water and my journal

5. *feeling like you have to be a certain way* - never be embarrassed of your anxiety. almost everyone experiences it, but they don't always show it. own it. talk about it. a couple months ago i had a job interview and my interviewer asked me if i was nervous, i truthfully replied with *"yes, i am"*, and then he asked me to take a deep breath with him and it was a breeze after that. sometimes simply pointing out the fact that you're anxious, is the recognition that your mind is needing to hear, so that you don't feel so trapped. when anxiety is knocking, open the door for that unwelcome guest and prove that you're not scared

sarah ciminillo

self-love and healing

naked

i won't overthink
and i won't assume

i'll just carry on
and leave baggage
like that
behind

- *ready to take flight*

sarah ciminillo

it's not always about how far you go
it's about how deep you go

you can walk two feet
and fall into
a place, a person, a book
and discover things about yourself
that you would've missed if you
kept walking

there's no rush
in your journey

naked

running with the wolves
brings a sense of freedom
and rebellion

but at the end of the day
it's not enough
for i have the appetite of a lion

i want mountains
and independence

sarah ciminillo

being a firm believer
in not forcing things
and also going for
what i want
leaves me floating
in space
around many stars
wishing for something
to happen

the science of healing

i think the tears that i shed
time and time again
watered a seed
inside of me
that started sprouting
before i even realized it
and suddenly
i was filled with
inspiration and hope
and i believe
thats the art
of growing as a person

sarah ciminillo

<u>temporarily numb</u>

those nights you went out
looking for fulfillment
when you only filled yourself with booze
and threw it up later
making you feel more empty
than you did before

fulfillment doesn't require emptying a bottle

<u>self-sabotage addict</u>

maybe
i keep pushing my limits
to the breaking point
seeing how far i can go
how badly i can mess up
so i can feel that high i get
from rising up again

sarah ciminillo

i really am tired of
holding onto them -
these balloons that are only sticking
around because i won't let them go

- *worries*

naked

self -realization
feels like
when i saw a shooting star
for the first time

amazed
eager
there within a blink
filled with butterflies

and it didn't matter
if no one else saw it
because i know
that *i* did

sarah ciminillo

darling
you're an ocean
full of
seashells
life
and mystery

don't be sad that
you didn't connect
with a puddle
he can't handle
your waves
and you're too good
for just ripples

naked

even plants
grow in the fog
your uncertainty
isn't wrong
being lost
doesn't mean
you are
it just means
that life is
raising the bar

sarah ciminillo

<u>discouragement is a seed</u>

let your passion and love
be acres wide
regardless of the times you were
cut down and burned
because if a forest
can grow back
then you can
too

naked

<u>your worth</u>

as humans
we tend to think
if feelings aren't
reciprocated
that our worth
becomes compromised

but i'm here to inform you
that if someone wants to buy something
then they will
no matter the cost
because they want it
if someone doesn't like the price
and decides not to buy it
that's their choice
that item won't decrease in value
or price
just because someone doesn't like it

and sure they can bargain
but that would require selling it
for less than what it truly is

don't settle for someone who doesn't see your value
don't settle for someone who tries to change your price

you're a good person

it's okay to give people chances
even when you're not totally sure about it

and it's okay to be let down

but don't think that you let yourself down

at the very least
you're a good person for giving someone a chance

naked

we don't get forever
and yet we fear it
in jobs
in relationships

wouldn't it make more sense
and give us all the more reason
to commit to them
to embrace them
because
we don't get forever

sarah ciminillo

<u>the world needs you</u>

you are like the sun my love
shining so bright that sometimes
people turn their eyes from you
because it may seem like too much for them

they can't help but to love the encompassing
warmth
they embrace it
soak it up
people anticipate the sun
and the undeniable energy it gives
without even knowing

so next time you feel under appreciated
or the odd one out
just know that your presence doesn't go
unnoticed
your presence impacts the rest of the world
even when no one is looking at you

naked

<u>what's a bad person?</u>

i'm flying high in a plane, overseeing the world - thinking about how we oversee flaws in one another. it makes me wonder, is anyone ever truly a bad person? we shuffle through personalities and versions of ourselves throughout our lifetime; making small mistakes, and sometimes big ones. fixing them, owning up to them, and turning into new people. whereas someone would see you as a bad person for the mistake you made, another person knows that it was a bump in the road for you. we're walking past versions of people in a certain moment - in the mall, on a plane, on a train. in our own home. we will never see that one version again - yet that either makes or breaks our perspective of that person. and don't you think that maybe our impression of a person, is a perspective that no longer exists? a view frozen in time - a fossil that shows what once was, but isn't any longer, because it has adapted to its surroundings and environment. which leads me to think that life isn't black and white - that the grey areas are where we exist but we choose when we want to be black and white. is anyone ever truly a bad person?

sarah ciminillo

<u>a girl's best friend</u>

i shine best
when i'm surrounded by darkness
those gutted feelings
and shrinking ceilings
press down on me
diamonds run down my cheeks
as days turn into weeks

and i shine
even when i don't know it

naked

the people
who convince you
that you're not

enough
educated
or beautiful

are the same people
who try to
convince themselves
that they are those things

- *robbery*

sarah ciminillo

and guess what?
it's okay
for people to
use your past
and insecurities
against you
because all
they are doing
is reusing
obstacles
that you've already
mastered

- *you can run that track backwards,*
  blindfolded, and look damn good doing it

naked

sometimes we don't do the things
we've been wanting to do
until we see someone else doing them
and succeeding at it
that's why we need each other

- *poetry community*

sarah ciminillo

i want to create
i want to love
i want to be loved
and i want to share that
with the world

naked

<u>smelling the roses</u>

today
i am grateful for
small things
i am grateful for
the colors of my room
and the way i sink into my bed
the way the sunlight
shoots in
and the messy bun on my head
for i longed for moments
like these
a year ago

- *feeling content*

sarah ciminillo

get serious about your passions
that excitement you get in your stomach
is part of you
not everyone gets that feeling when they think
about your specific passion
everything that you are
and everything that has happened to you
has given you the perfect environment to
become what you're supposed to be

you were put on this earth
at this specific time
with your talents and passions engraved into
you
never settle with the thought
that anyone can do what you do

everyone has something special to offer

you just have to believe

naked

falling in love

love is

not the words
or person
that we fall for

but it's the sensation
of home
and our hearts
latch onto that
signaling
our minds
to stay

naked

<u>modern refreshments</u>

"i want to hang out with you sober"
poured from your lips
and hydrated my soul

sarah ciminillo

somewhere down the line
it was believed that love
is when we give ourselves to someone

but love isn't selfish like that

love is when we share ourselves
with someone else
it's enjoying a personality so much
that we start to imagine a future with it
and couldn't bare the idea of hurting it

sometimes our experiences with love
feels a lot like death in the sense that
a past love is set in stone
that our beliefs can never change about love
because it exists in a tomb somewhere in the past

but love isn't dark like that

love is light and ever-changing
love is repeated new feelings
it's using past experiences to build on

our losses only make us wise
and that's why love never dies

naked

<u>two fireflies</u>

there was never a dull moment with you
even though dullness was all that moment had
to give
we gave it meaning

sarah ciminillo

i've never truly been in love
until i met you
with you i learned that love existed
in the cracks of sidewalks
in the coffee shop
in the park when it was hot

it existed when we weren't doing anything
besides being ourselves

naked

tell me
how do i think
straight
with the curve of
your lips
demanding
to be twisted
with mine

- *lingering lust*

sarah ciminillo

<u>wholesome</u>

be with the person
whose gravity pulls you
down to earth
but makes you feel
like the universe

naked

my lips ran out of words
as if they were preparing

and my mind had
just one thought
as if it never has many

- *kiss me*

sarah ciminillo

your arms were wrapped
so tightly around me
that i couldn't recall
any sort of fear
that i previously had
about anything

- *the power of touch*

naked

i am
infatuated by
you

i love you
sits in the back of
my head
becoming watered
each time we
exchange glimpses
words
and touches

sarah ciminillo

<u>mermaid soul</u>

i'm sick of minnows
and sick of sand
take my hand
and i'll show you
how deep we could go
i'll show you a world
you've never known

naked

you kissed my shoulder
in a moonlit room
and then i understood
how stars were made

- *a fire that is no longer constrained*

sarah ciminillo

show me a song
and i'll listen to it
everyday
just to understand
how it makes you feel

tell me about your adventures
and i'll try to envision them in my head

these are things i do without effort

this is when i know it is real

naked

soft yet edgy
my feelings for you
in a frenzy

for once
i'm freed from my past
you feel like the next
and the last

sarah ciminillo

i cannot decide
what is more intimate -
a man touching my body
or a man seeing me before i lay my head to rest
no make-up on
hair a mess
braless

closing my eyes
as i slip away
limbs intertwining
as we lay

it is when
i am most vulnerable
and at peace
a state that not
everyone gets to see

naked

you and i
are a riddle
because
we are still
so little
but i'd be
lying
if a little
part of me
didn't want
to be riddled
with you
so maybe
you can meet me
somewhere in
the mixed up
middle

sarah ciminillo

i want a love
that consumes me

like every poetry book i've read
like every exchange of smiles i've had
like every belly laughter i've felt

i want my body to know it

naked

quarantine journals

sarah ciminillo

it's in his stupid eyes
and my unachievable goodbyes
it's in the shape of his lips when he laughs
how we talk on the phone
when i take baths

he never upsets me - only inspires
meeting him has been a trail of fires
i'm heating up but also creating danger
i broke up with my boyfriend for liking a stranger

truly a stupid girl with a
foolish heart
friend or lover?
i can never tell them apart

my days are now
purple laced with gold
our story is poetry
that i will tell when i'm old

sharing art and late night talks on the phone
i can't have you, yet
this is the greatest love i've ever known

naked

<u>this world we live in is something new</u>

i know the days have been rainy
and there haven't been many colors
it's okay to stay under the covers

it's okay that your
motivation isn't there
it's okay to keep
your face bare

it's okay to grow tired
of the same routine
life is like a film
we crave the next scene

it's okay to feel lost
like you don't know what you're doing
in fact it's good
because its your mind renewing

it's okay to not have the energy
to speak
it's okay not to know
the day of the week

you're diving into yourself
you're being true to you

sarah ciminillo

and i just want to say
that i'm so proud of you

naked

honest and so kind
crowded room, your eyes - i find
come near, my mirror

day 6 quarantine

it's not fair
it's not fair that you tell me that i'm pretty
that my eyes make you feel adored
it's not fair that you send me your poetry - *and it's good*
it's not fair that your eyes and smile grab my soul
it's not fair that i melt

it's not fair that i expect myself to not fall in love with you
it's not fair that i'm living in our messages and phone calls

it's not fair that i want someone i can't have

naked

i have to keep
our love
a secret
during quarantine
when i don't have
any human interaction
except you
and sometimes
i wonder
if any of it
is even real

   - *the twilight zone*

day 11 quarantine

*"just be you. i like you with your feelings,
please do not protect me from mine"*
he said

we are forced to live day by day
so that's exactly what i'm going to keep doing
with him
i'm going to keep my focus on my journey
stay true to my feelings
and not worry about his
because if i do
if i go down that road
i'll go too far
like i always do
and lose sight of my own
i'll lose myself

    but some days

                         *i feel as though
i already have*

naked

a timeless love

our walks on sunny trails should become a
painting in a museum
our long talks under the shaded trees should
become a poetry book for all to read when they
need encouragement or laughs
our first kiss in the car when it rained should
become a scene in a movie
*although i'm not sure that they could capture the
passion tingling through every square inch of my
body*
our midnight phone calls should become a
novel describing the lives of two people who,
despite their journeys, met each other and loved
each other unconditionally
our love making should be sculpted into a piece
that describes what it's like when you become
one with another human being

a timeless love
should be made into all the forms of art
hanging around us
reminding us that when love is real
that even when you think you can't have
someone
the universe will surprise you

sarah ciminillo

we passed a bottle of red
back and forth
touching it to our lips
and then touching each others
hands traveling and us
becoming lovers

naked

<u>day 17 of quarantine</u>

last night i had my first panic attack i've had in months, and it wasn't chill. but i feel like i got down to the roots and removed it the best way i could.
i was in the bath tub, and the stiff numbness sets in my hands. i was scared.
i clench my fists and take huge deep breaths. my hands were stuck in fist form, as if they turned to stone. i wanted to punch my wall. for the first time i was more angry than afraid with myself, because i thought i worked through these episodes, that i was done with them. but running through my mind were all the deaths of people and the unpredictability of the virus. the uncertainty of my life ever going back to normal. of anyone's life going back to normal. i felt empty, alone, afraid.

i'm not afraid
i didn't get this "breathe" tattoo for nothing

i was saying these things out loud like a crazy person. then the tingles started to slowly subside. my hands were then shaking - like i just had three cups of coffee on an empty stomach.

hands are still clenched and i'm sitting in fetal position. naked in the bathtub. as bare as I can be, my eyes start to become the water source for my tub.
i know this is the end of the attack.
feeling weak, i lay back - my muscles feel like they just went through a marathon.
i sip my vodka and cranberry.
i felt accomplished.
i made it through - *and totally alone.*

naked

i tasted your love
raw yet bold made me unfold
connection of eyes

sarah ciminillo

day 19 quarantine

my sister greeted me with a clementine in bed
so sweet
she also made breakfast and i was fortunate
enough to eat it with the sun
i'm wearing my favorite butterfly crop-top and
shorts
it's just the perfect weather for it

- *little gratitudes*

naked

<u>day 31 quarantine</u>

something happened yesterday -
i called my dad
it's something i had been thinking about for a while
and it wasn't as scary as i thought it would be
it was half the battle
the other half is going to see him
i feel as ready as i'll ever be to do it
i finally believe and love myself enough to be considered untouchable by the person who took those things away many years ago

believing in oneself is not given, you have to choose it - work towards it
finding this new love during quarantine has made me realize that
not for any particular reason
but just by him being himself
kind, real, understanding, and a doer of all things

there is something so inspiring and beautiful about someone who has had a tough journey too
and shows vulnerability and pure kindness

a person who gives others a chance despite what their opinions say

i don't think he even knows the impact he has made on my life
if and when the dynamic between us changes
he will forever go down

in this book
in my heart

as someone who helped me - by simply believing in me

i didn't know what that felt like until i met him

naked

a trigger environment
for my anxiety is the car
something about
the small space
and lack of fresh air
makes me feel like
i'm in a shrinking box

so when i got in his car
and saw those kind eyes
and smile that hugs my soul
it made me feel guilty
that it wasn't enough
to defeat my anxiety
because eyes and smiles
as precious and genuine
as his
should never ever
go unappreciated

i soaked them up like
rays from the sun
next thing i knew
i was hot
and by the way he
was looking at me
i knew that he could read
every sign my body

was expressing

he asked for my hand
i rejected the offer
as i wiped my palms
on my pants
i take a deep breath
and exhale with words
that seemed like the
only ones i knew
*"i need to get out
of this car"*

he replies with
*"i'll take
the next
exit"*

we stop at
a gas station
paired with a
liquor store
perfect
i thought

he reminded me
that at any point
i can change my

naked

mind
and go home
if that would
make me more
comfortable
and that maybe
i should get out
and walk around

he goes inside
the liquor store
i get out
and lean against
the car like a
character from a
road trip movie

i scroll on my phone
with zombie eyes
not really looking at
or reading anything
just trying to seem
like i'm normal

he returns
and hugs me
and reveals
shooters of vodka

and i exhale with
relief
hoping he wouldn't
judge me for being
so relieved

he laughs
and says
*"i got some
for me too"*

we laugh
and i slowly
float back
down to earth
thankful to know
such a mindful
person

naked

quarantine has taken a lot
from me, from everyone

>   social outings
>   concerts
>   a hug from my mother - *an irreplaceable*
>   *feeling*

but i wouldn't have gained something without it

i fell in love with someone
that you're not
supposed to fall in love with
because of current roles and timing
let alone, during quarantine
our odds were very much
stacked against us

>   *yet*

we prevailed
i don't take that lightly

it's not ideal that
i fell in love with him
time is clearly not
on our side

but our timelines
crossed
just that one time
and we haven't stopped
sharing eyes and words
since

i found out what
it means to love
unconditionally
i'm not
receiving anything
from him

just him

a secret garden
that i visit
that i admire
that i confide to
that i water
that i want to pick and
take home
with me
but that i love
too much
to do that to
all i have

naked

is my gratitude
my woeful eyes
and a love
that i am
terrified and
fascinated
by

sarah ciminillo

i have three empty wine bottles
on my window sill

the first one we drank
was on a golf course
under the moon

the second one we drank
was on a grassy meadow
under a tree

the third one we drank
was on my bed
under the blankets

and i look at them
like trophies

three empty wine bottles
filled with
memories
and you

naked

if i had to guess what depression feels like, i'd
say it feels a lot like quarantine.
i can see why people become depressed when
they're inactive and unable to leave their house.
i don't even know what day of quarantine it is,
and as much as i love my lavender colored walls
and feather down comforter, i don't feel at ease.
i crack my window for some cool, fresh air.
words and memories are bouncing around my
room as i scan around for my cat - *lana.* she is
sitting in my window sill, and i wonder how she
does that everyday for hours.
i feel like i'm living in the twilight zone; like
everything is on pause and in a fog, but looks
the same.
which in turn, makes everything else in my life
feel like it's on pause too.
my writing.
my dreams.
my goals.
i feel like i'm wasting valuable time to do art
and create what i've been putting off for
months. but my heart isn't in it right now; my
heart is slightly breaking and mending at the
same time.
and so, i'm not going to do anything besides
listen to my heart.

sarah ciminillo

there's a time to *just feel*, and then there's a time to *create*.
an artist is not an artist, without *both*.
and right now, i'm just going to feel.

naked

our timelines have overlapped many times
before
in other lives
i know this by how we speak with our eyes

every heart that i've broke
every pillow that i've soaked
every night when i laid down and wondered
what words should've spoke
were the grains of sand in the hourglass

falling

    down to

        meeting

            you

sarah ciminillo

i've noticed during quarantine
that my boundaries have been less appealing
and more challenging
to listen to
any excuse i have to feel something
good or bad
i'll use it
and that's abusive
there will be times when life is a bore
doesn't mean i should reopen
a past door

naked

what's wrong?

i feel like a compass
searching for my path
but my path doesn't exist yet
so i'm just spinning
i'm dizzy from all the
possibilities
staying in one spot
unable to move

i want to run through the forest
and feel sea foam on my feet
kiss the lips of someone sweet

i want to explore my paths

sarah ciminillo

when quarantine started, my only mindset was wondering when it would end. i was upset with the world and the way things were put to a halt in my life. i had recently started a new job that i fell in love with, i was in a good place mentally, and i finally felt like i was on a path that i was sure about. and feeling so sure about anything is a rare shooting star moment; a feeling that just happens, and you're not entirely sure where it came from, but you feel it in your heart.
i was staying in bed a lot. i felt disconnected and unsure about everything. fear was behind the scenes, taking credit at the end of the day.
but then something happened. i felt a type of love that exists throughout my whole body, and had experiences that i wouldn't trade for anything. experiences that would have never happened if quarantine didn't happen. i didn't think i would ever be grateful for quarantine, but here i am.
here i am missing quarantine. missing the time i shared with him, and sad with the current reality that i wanted to have back so badly. angry that it no longer feels like it's enough. but alas, forever thankful that i was gifted his love and time.
and i think life will always be unfair like that. we will strive, work hard, feel a new love, and

naked

yet it will not be promised. but the silver lining is the experiences we get from them, and the promise of new ones to come.
we don't know why things happen the way they do, and we don't know a blessing in disguise until after the fact; so trust the path even when it's rocky and you can't find your shoes. it's a necessary part of your journey - the struggles, the tears, the heartbreak, the anxieties - are all worth the love and art.

it's how i was able to create this book.

sarah ciminillo

Made in the USA
Monee, IL
03 July 2021